Dark Psychology Handbook

Best Guide for how to understand and influence people using Mind Control, Manipulation Complete Step by Step Guide

Julia Smith

© Copyright 2021 by Julia Smith

- All rights reserved.

The following Book is reproduced below with the goal of providing information that is as accurate and reliable as possible. Regardless, purchasing this Book can be seen as consent to the fact that both the publisher and the author of this book are in no way experts on the topics discussed within and that any recommendations or suggestions that are made herein are for entertainment purposes only. Professionals should be consulted as needed prior to undertaking any of the action endorsed herein.

This declaration is deemed fair and valid by both the American Bar Association and the Committee of Publishers Association and is legally binding throughout the United States.

Furthermore, the transmission, duplication, or reproduction of any of the following work including specific information will be considered an illegal act irrespective of if it is done electronically or in print. This extends to creating a secondary or tertiary copy of the work or a recorded copy and is only allowed with the express written consent from the Publisher. All additional right reserved.

The information in the following pages is broadly considered a truthful and accurate account of facts and as such, any inattention, use, or misuse of the information in question by the reader will render any resulting actions solely under their purview. There are no scenarios in which the publisher or the original author of this work can be in any fashion deemed liable for any hardship or damages that may befall them after undertaking information described herein.

Additionally, the information in the following pages is intended only for informational purposes and should thus be thought of as universal. As befitting its nature, it is presented without assurance regarding its prolonged validity or interim quality. Trademarks that are mentioned are done without written consent and can in no way be considered an endorsement from the trademark holder.

Table of Contents

CHAPTER ONE:

THE ART OF PERSUASION

Endeavors to convince might be contentious or non-pugnacious. Non-factious methods for influence incorporate creation eyes, brushing hands, and putting a decent dinner onto the table.

Be that as it may, significantly more typical, particularly in the open circle, is the utilization of talk, which is the craft of convincing talking or composing.

Barack Obama got himself chose and reappointed to the White House less by the power of his contentions than by his considerable explanatory aptitudes. The premise of his celebrated 'Yes we can' shtick, for instance, is the explanatory gadget of epistrophe (see later).

Explanatory gadgets are likewise wonderful gadgets that can be utilized to improve just as to convince. Governmental issues aside, explanatory gadgets—as I will show you—underlie all our preferred sonnets and tunes and articulations.

I arrange the best explanatory gadgets into only eight gatherings: sound reiteration, word redundancy, thought or structure redundancy, surprising structure, language games, resistance and logical inconsistency, diversion, and symbolism.

I'll presently take you through these eight gatherings and attempt to clarify the brain research of every one. (The models I use are referenced at the foot of the article.)

1. Sound redundancy

The redundancy of a sound or sounds can create a satisfying feeling of agreement. It can likewise quietly interface or stress significant words or thoughts. There are two significant types of sound reiteration: consonance and similar sounding word usage.

Consonance is the reiteration of a similar consonant sound, as in, for instance,

Rap dismisses my cassette player, discharges shot/Whether Jew or gentile I rank top percentile

Similar sounding word usage is a type of consonance including a similar consonant sound toward the start of each word or focused on syllable.

Snooping around can lead to unexpected trouble.

Sibilance is a type of consonance including the redundancy of sibilant sounds, for example,/s/and/sh/. Sibilance is quieting and erotic, though similar sounding word usage on a hard stable creates a totally unique impact.

What's more, the luxurious tragic dubious stirring of each purple drapery...

2. Word redundancy

Word redundancy can make similar sounding word usage, beat or coherence, accentuation, association, and movement.

Words can be rehashed in a few different ways.

Most clearly, a word can be rehashed in prompt progression (epizeuxis), as in, for instance:

O dull, dim, dim, in the midst of the blast of early afternoon

Or on the other hand it tends to be rehashed after a couple of mediating words (diacope) or toward the start and end of a statement or line (epanalepsis).

Bond, James Bond

The lord is dead, long live the ruler!

Romeo, Romeo, wherefore craftsmanship thou my Romeo?

Or on the other hand it tends to be conveyed opposite one condition or line to the following, with the word that closes one provision or line starting the following (anadiplosis). This brings out key thoughts and their association, instilling the recommendation with something like the quality and certainty of hard, deductive rationale.

We likewise cheer in our sufferings, since we realize that enduring produces persistence; steadiness, character; and character, trust. Furthermore, trust doesn't disillusion us.

Just as single words, gatherings of words can be rehashed, either toward the start of progressive statements or lines (anaphora), or toward the finish of progressive provisos or lines (epistrophe/epiphora).

There is no Negro issue. There is no Southern issue. There is no Northern issue. There is just an American issue.

On the off chance that you need to toss the kitchen sink at it, you can consolidate anaphora with epistrophe (symploce).

When there is discussion of contempt, let us stand up and talk against it. When there is discussion of viciousness, let us stand up and talk against it.

In this specific model, the reiteration passes on assurance, resolve, and harmony.

3. Thought or structure reiteration

The reiteration of a thought or structure can, whenever utilized effectively, add extravagance and reverberation to articulation. It can likewise include accentuation; make request, cadence, and movement; and evoke an all out idea.

How about we start with redundancy, which is the reiteration of a similar thought inside a line.

With noxiousness toward none, with foundation for all.

Pleonasm is a kind of redundancy including the utilization of a greater number of words than is vital for clear articulation.

I am the Alpha and the Omega, the First and the Last, the Beginning and the End.

The last model is a blend of pleonasm and parallelism, which includes utilizing a comparable linguistic structure in a couple or arrangement of related words, statements, or lines. Three equal words, provisos, or lines establishes a tricolon, which is an especially compelling sort of isocolon.

Distraught, terrible, and perilous to know

Auxiliary or linguistic equals can be featured by methods for basic inversion (chiasmus).

Yet, numerous that are first will be last; and the last will be first.

4. Unordinary structure

An unordinary structure draws consideration and can likewise make a move in accentuation.

Hyperbaton is the adjustment of the typical request of the words in a sentence, or the partition of words that ordinarily go together. There are a few kinds. Anastrophe includes reversal of standard word request. Hypallage includes transference of properties from their legitimate subjects to other people. Hysteron proteron includes reversal of regular sequence.

Over the oceans to stand (anastrophe)

Irate crown of rulers (hypallage)

Allow us to bite the dust, and surge into the main part of the battle. (hysteron proteron)

Zeugma is the joining of at least two pieces of a sentence with a solitary action word (or now and then a thing). Contingent on the situation of the action word (toward the start, in the center, or toward the end), a zeugma is either a prozeugma, mesozeugma, or hypozeugma. Here is a case of a mesozeugma:

What a disgrace is this, that neither any expectation of remuneration, nor feare of rebuke could anything move him, neither the influence of his companions, nor the adoration for his nation.

Syllepsis is a sort of zeugma where a solitary word concurs syntactically with at least two different words, however semantically with just one.

She brought down her measures by raising her glass, her mental fortitude, her eyes, and his expectations.

Hypozeuxis is the converse of zeugma, wherein each subject is appended to its own action word. The accompanying, from Churchill, is additionally a case of anaphora

We will battle on the sea shores. We will battle on the arrival grounds. We will battle in the fields, and in the lanes, we will battle in the slopes. We will never give up!

5. Language games

Language games, for example, quips and conscious mix-ups can cause to notice an expression or thought, or essentially raise a grin, by making new and regularly silly pictures and affiliations.

They can likewise offer ascent to a clear picture, make vagueness, and propose earnestness and even energy.

A quip (or paronomasia) is a figure of speech that sound the same, or on a word that has more than one importance.

Do inn administrators land board with their positions?

A canine brought forth young doggies close to the street and was refered to for littering.

She is decent from far, yet a long way from pleasant.

Catachresis is the purposeful abuse of a word or manner of expression, for instance, utilizing single word for another, or stressing or blending similitudes.

To take arms against an ocean of difficulties...

'Tis most profound winter in Lord Timon's tote

Antitimeria is the purposeful abuse of a word as though it were an individual from an alternate word class, regularly a thing for an action word.

I'll unhair thy head.

Enallage is the purposeful and successful utilization of wrong sentence structure.

Let him kiss me with the kisses of his mouth, for thy love is superior to wine.

Love me delicate, love me valid

6. Restriction and logical inconsistency

The utilization of restriction or logical inconsistency causes to notice itself, powers thought, can be hilarious, and can propose movement and fruition.

An ironic expression is a juxtaposition of words which from the start sight appears to be conflicting or confused. A mystery is like a paradoxical expression, yet less conservative.

Make flurry gradually

What a pity that adolescent must be squandered on the youthful.

Antiphrasis is the utilization of a word in a setting where it implies its inverse.

A mammoth of five foot three inches

Direct opposite is the utilization of a couple of contrary energies for differentiating impact. A progression of absolute opposites is known as a movement.

An opportunity to be conceived, and an opportunity to pass on; an opportunity to plant, and an opportunity to cull up what is planted; an opportunity to kill, and an opportunity to recuperate…

7. Aversion

Aversion works by painting an image, or conjuring up an unpredictable thought, with only a couple of very much picked words.

Hendiadys is the juxtaposition of two words, and hendriatris of three.

Dieu et mon droit

Sex, medications, and rock'n'roll

Lock, stock, and barrel

The last model is likewise a merism, which includes listing the parts to mean the entirety. Here's another merism:

For better for more terrible, for more extravagant for less fortunate, in infection and in wellbeing...

8. Symbolism

Clearly, symbolism works by conjuring up a specific picture.

Metonymy is the naming of a thing or idea by something else that is firmly connected with it.

Bringing down Street

The White House

The pen is mightier than the sword

Antonomasia, a sort of metonymy, is the utilization of a word or expression or designation instead of an appropriate name.

The Divine Teacher (Plato)

The Master of Those Who Know (Aristotle)

The Subtle Doctor (Duns Scotus)

Synedoche, which is like metonymy, is the naming of a thing or idea by one of its parts.

A couple of hands

Longshanks

A couple of definite words

With talk, it isn't (only) the rationale, however the excellence and persuasiveness and striking quality that does the convincing.

In Plato's Lysis, Socrates says that excellence 'is surely a delicate, smooth, elusive thing, and along these lines of a nature which effectively slips in and penetrates our spirits.'

You will, obviously, have seen the exotic sibilance of that state.

Influence is the demonstration of persuading somebody to change their convictions or accomplish something you recommend. Influence has frequently been depicted as a sensitive type of workmanship, however what precisely makes it so incredible? Understanding the craft of influence can not just assist you with figuring out how to impact others; it can likewise make you increasingly mindful of the procedures others may use to attempt to change your convictions and practices.

Why Persuasion Is an Art

To comprehend the specialty of influence, you should initially comprehend the more extensive meaning of craftsmanship. Craftsmanship is both a procedure and item that:

- Communicates forceful feeling
- Is mentally testing
- Is intricate and intelligible
- Passes on complex messages
- Shows an individual perspective
- Is unique

23

- Produces an item or execution that requires a high level of ability

In spite of the fact that it is clear how all the highlights above apply to such works of art as painting and performing music, not all apply to the specialty of influence. Influence isn't a fine art in a similar sense as painting or music, but instead includes the finely tuned imaginative abilities or craft of language and correspondence. Be that as it may, influence includes a portion of the characteristics of progressively conventional fine arts. It's mentally testing, mind boggling, expressive, and totally valid to your character.

What Is the Point of Persuasion?

You may ask why you should try to figure out how to convince others. You may even consider such a "workmanship" to be wicked or manipulative. Nonetheless, in all actuality each effective individual has, one after another or another, been in a position where they needed to convince somebody of something. For example, the vast majority need to convince a business to recruit them before they can even start to work and acquire cash.

Influence goes through numerous human undertakings. Sales reps convince individuals to purchase items or administrations. Legislators convince individuals to help and decision in favor of them. Scalawags convince individuals to succumb to tricks and go through cash they don't have. You may convince your educator to let you take a cosmetics test, convince your better half or beau to wed you, or convince somebody to help with your volunteer program. Truth be told, it's really elusive individuals completing anything at all without some type of influence.

So whether you ought to learn better influence strategies truly isn't an inquiry. The inquiry is the reason you haven't done so as of now.

Variables to Consider in the Art of Persuasion

Anybody can rehearse the craft of influence. Be that as it may, it takes devotion to figure out how to do it adequately. A few people appear to have a talent for persuading individuals to see things their way. In case you're thinking that its hard to learn, it's not the apocalypse. You can, and will, figure out how to ace this workmanship. The following are a few variables to consider before you attempt to convince someone of something:

Evaluate How Easy the Persuasion Will Be. You can start by discovering how troublesome it will be to prevail upon your crowd. Specialists have discovered a few factors that impact how simple it very well may be to persuade somebody regarding something. You simply need to follow the correct rules and methods.

Gathering Membership. On the off chance that you're an individual from a gathering, at that point you're factually more averse to be persuaded of subjects or thoughts that conflict with the perspectives on your individual gathering individuals. The presence of the gathering and your devotion to it will in general fortify your purpose to stay with their variant of reality, regardless of whether it's totally erroneous.

Low Self-Esteem. Individuals with low confidence are measurably far simpler to persuade than those with higher confidence. This is probably in light of the fact that they will in general worth others' suppositions more than they do their own. The greatest test you'll need to look here is deciding the degree of confidence of the individual you're attempting to convince. You can frequently do this by breaking down components, for example, body pose, certainty of tone, and pledge to your crowd's own perspective.

Hindrance of Aggression. In the event that you don't prefer to show animosity, at that point you're bound to be overwhelmed by a smooth talker who is familiar with the craft of influence. Regardless of whether they cause you to feel awkward about whatever they're attempting to persuade you regarding, absence of hostility will make it simpler for them to influence your assessments. Individuals who aren't inclined to demonstrating animosity as a rule don't challenge what the other individual is stating.

Burdensome Tendencies. Research shows that individuals who are discouraged are all the more effectively persuaded to acknowledge another person's perspectives over their own. This is to a great extent because of elements like absence of hostility and confidence, as referenced previously. Nonetheless, you may locate that a few people who experience the ill effects of sorrow may not really be convinced by you, yet just concur with you to keep away from struggle.

Social Inadequacy. The individuals who view themselves as socially insufficient will in general be all the more handily convinced. Regardless of whether they're no more socially maladroit than others, the way that they see themselves that way drives them to put the weight of discussion on the individual they're cooperating with. This makes it simpler for that individual to convince them without challenge.

Since you realize a few components to consider before endeavoring to convince somebody, how about we investigate the procedure of influence.

Step by step instructions to Practice Persuasion: A Process

Getting the Right Introduction

It is incredibly hard to persuade an outsider of something. For example, salesmen loathe cold pitching since they never know the kind of individual they're managing on the opposite end. They don't have a clue about their qualities, inclinations, or whether they have a place with a gathering that is against what/how they are selling. Similarly as significantly, the individual called doesn't have a clue, and trust, the salesman.

In the event that you can get a presentation from a shared companion or associate, you have a greatly improved possibility of convincing somebody to receive your perspective. In the event that you can't get a presentation, it assists with setting yourself up for anything before you endeavor influence. This is the place fantastic tuning in and relational abilities enter the image.

The Value of Listening

At the point when you listen first, you assemble the data you have to make a customized pitch that will sound good to the individual you're attempting to convince. Canny political competitors don't simply appear at your entryway and begin addressing you. Rather, they ordinarily pose a few inquiries about your perspectives to locate a beginning stage for their influence. Really perfect system, isn't that so?

Notwithstanding the data you gain from tuning in, you make the feeling that you esteem the other individual and regard their convictions. Thusly, they're bound to size up you and tune in to what you need to state.

Being Agreeable When You Don't Agree

It's essential to communicate concurrence with the individual you're attempting to convince as frequently as could be expected under the circumstances. This shows you regard them and are receptive. Everybody needs to be thought of as savvy, so on the off chance that you discredit all that somebody says, they're probably going to excuse you. Obviously, you can't concur with anybody on everything, nor do you need to. In the event that you did, you wouldn't have the option to persuade your crowd to change their position. What you can do, be that as it may, is have a pleasing mentality that recognizes the thinking behind what they accept and the decisions they've made.

Nuance Is Crucial

On the off chance that you can say precisely what you need somebody to accept and they promptly trust it, there isn't a lot of a requirement for influence. All the more generally, you have to show them in inconspicuous manners why your perspective is right. There are a wide range of influence procedures to utilize, yet the best are those that aren't explicit or self-evident. Rather, they're based on drawing correlations, narrating, and perceiving the other individual and where they stand.

Influence and Morals

The craft of influence requires persistence and duty to the procedure. In the event that it involved just saying "Trust me!" there wouldn't be a lot of influence included. So as to alter somebody's perspective, you have to set aside the effort to build up your contentions and clarify your reason, unobtrusively and reliably. On the off chance that it's a basic message, it probably won't take long to convey. Be that as it may, in the event that you need to convey something increasingly mind boggling, you should show restraint toward your crowd and keep them locked in.

Whose Conclusion Matters?

At the point when you attract your contention to a nearby, you may introduce your decision as the clearly right one. Be that as it may, individuals are all the more handily convinced in the event that they accept they're arriving at their own determination regarding a matter. They need to accept that it's their plan to change their perspectives, convictions, or activities. The uplifting news is, on the off chance that you've introduced your contention such that sounds good to your crowd, they'll likely accept that their adjustment in believing was their own choice. Subsequently, they'll be bound to keep on clutching that assessment and, all the more significantly, follow up on it.

Moral Concerns

There are a couple of moral quandaries to consider on the off chance that you choose you're going to rehearse the specialty of influence. Numerous individuals have utilized influence methods malignantly to damage or exploit others. Before you attempt to persuade somebody to concur with you, consider what the effect on them will be on the off chance that you succeed.

Will that individual pick up or lose? Is it to their greatest advantage to acknowledge what you bring to the table?

Undue impact is a lawful term that implies you convince somebody to act in opposition to their own unrestrained choice or without thoughtfulness regarding the results. This turns into an issue when somebody is weakened somehow or another and incapable to settle on their own choices. For instance, a parental figure may persuade a more seasoned grown-up to change their will and leave everything to them. In case you're thinking about rehearsing the craft of influence, it's an ethical basic to evade undue impact. It will likewise keep you out of legitimate difficulty.

Adulterating Evidence

Regardless of whether you're in court or making a post via web-based networking media, it's inappropriate to introduce misrepresented articulations, reports, or pictures to demonstrate your point. On the off chance that you need to be capable and kind in your act of influence, you have to ensure that the proof or supporting data you're introducing is, as far as you could possibly know, exact and real.

Propagating Scams

Individuals who utilize their familiarity of influence to trick others regularly couldn't care less whether what they're doing is harming others. Regularly, the individuals they wind up persuading at that point endeavor to persuade others regarding something very similar without understanding that they've been conned. To abstain from sustaining the tricks of others, it's essential to get your realities straight and consistently remain alarm to the chance of double dealing.

So Is Persuasion Good or Bad?

Like some other type of workmanship, influence is neither positive nor negative all by itself. It is the manner by which you utilize the craft of influence, and for what reason, that decides if you're contributing something advantageous to the world.

The powerlessness to convince others can be an extraordinary impediment throughout everyday life. You may experience difficulty finding a new line of work, purchasing a home, or making the following stride in your relationship. Then again, you may view that you're as excessively effortlessly persuaded and succumb to each trick introduced to you. Assuming this is the case, there are a few different ways to diminish your defenselessness to succumbing to each smooth please. An advisor can assist you with building your confidence, improve your social aptitudes, and even figure out how to deal with your downturn. These variables will make you less powerless against trickiness.

Looking for Guidance

You can converse with an authorized advisor at BetterHelp to get the assistance you need. Online treatment is moderate, advantageous, private, and can assist you with revealing your shrouded qualities. Regardless of whether you have to figure out how to be progressively influential or to examine the influence strategies of others, treatment can have a significant effect. You can find out about the two sides of the specialty of influence all around ok to both get what you need all the more effectively and ensure yourself. You have the right to be glad allowed us to help. The following are a few audits of BetterHelp advisors from individuals who became more beneficial and increasingly talented through treatment.

Guide Reviews

"In the limited ability to focus 9 months, Shonnie has gotten like probably the closest companion. From the outset, I was wary of doing treatment since I'm "mentally sound". A couple of difficulties in my own life drove me to attempt treatment for a month. Presently I think of it as a significant piece of my development as an agent and pioneer inside my locale. Much obliged to you Shonnie for being so useful during the ongoing troubles; I am fortunate to have discovered you!"

"Tyson truly got me out with my downturn by discovering what my objectives were throughout everyday life, particularly around my vocation and family. He left me with procedures and activities that have truly helped me watch negative considerations and break their cycles. I have really experienced a valid, positive change in my life because of Tyson. Enthusiastically suggest!"

The craft of influence is a dominance of correspondence systems that can assist you with arriving at your objectives by persuading others regarding your perspective. It can likewise be hard to distinguish, particularly from somebody who's conversant in it. With the tips and rules above, you'll be well on your way toward turning into an ace of influence and one who is shielded from being exploited by different experts. Venture out.

Thoughts are the money of the twenty-first century. The capacity to convince, to change hearts and brains, is maybe the single most prominent expertise that will give you a serious edge in the information economy — an age where thoughts matter like never before.

A few financial specialists accept that influence is answerable for producing one-quarter or a greater amount of America's absolute national pay. As our economy has developed from an agrarian to a mechanical to an information based one, fruitful individuals in almost every calling have gotten those fit for persuading others to make a move on their thoughts. Consider the job of influence in our every day lives:

- Business visionaries convince financial specialists to back their new companies.
- Occupation competitors convince selection representatives to employ them.
- Government officials convince individuals to decide in favor of them.
- Pioneers convince representatives to make explicit plans of move.
- Presidents convince experts to compose ideal reports about their organizations.
- Sales reps convince clients to pick their item over a contender's contribution.

———

To put it plainly, influence is not, at this point a "delicate aptitude"— it is a principal expertise that can assist you with drawing in speculators, sell items, manufacture brands, motivate groups, and trigger developments. Influence is so essential to very rich person Warren Buffett that the main recognition he gladly shows in his office is an open talking testament from a Dale Carnegie course. He once told business understudies that improving their relational abilities would help their expert incentive by half — in a split second.

Words and thoughts made the cutting edge world, and words and thoughts can possibly make you a star in your field, as long as you can convince another person to follow up on them. Following the strategies of one old Greek savant can help.

Over 2,000 years back Aristotle sketched out a recipe on the best way to ace the specialty of influence in his work Rhetoric. Numerous incredible communicators have utilized it all through the ages to convey probably the most compelling talks, introductions, and offer their thoughts with the world.

To turn into an ace of influence yourself and effectively sell your own thoughts, take a stab at utilizing these five explanatory gadgets that Aristotle recognized in your next discourse or introduction:

1) Ethos or "Character"

To me, ethos speaks to the piece of a discourse or introduction when your crowd increases some understanding into your validity. Aristotle accepted that if a speaker's activities didn't back their words, they would lose validity, and eventually, debilitate their contention.

For instance, in a now well known TED Talk on transforming the criminal equity framework, Human Rights Attorney Bryan Stevenson starts, "I invest a large portion of my energy in correctional facilities, in jails, waiting for capital punishment. I invest the greater part of my energy in exceptionally low-salary networks in the ventures and places where there's a lot of misery." You'll notice that Stevenson doesn't list his degrees, achievements, and grants like he may on a list of qualifications. Rather, he builds up his character for those in the crowd who don't have any acquaintance with him. Thusly, he is building a feeling of trust among himself and his audience members.

As people, we are designed to scan for motivations to confide in someone else, and we do so rapidly. All things considered, our predecessors had a moment to decide if an outsider was companion or enemy. A straightforward update that you are focused on the government assistance of others will construct your validity before you spread out your contention.

2) Logos or "Reason"

When ethos is set up, it's a great opportunity to make an intelligent intrigue to reason. For what reason should your crowd care about your thought? In the event that it will set aside your crowd cash, for instance, they'll need to realize the amount it will spare them and how the investment funds will be practiced. A similar thinking applies to bringing in cash. By what means will your thought help your audience members gain a benefit? What steps do they need to take straightaway? These are for the most part consistent interests that will assist you with picking up help. Use information, proof, and realities to frame a sound contention.

3) Pathos or "Feeling"

As indicated by Aristotle, influence can't happen without feeling. Individuals are moved to activity by how a speaker causes them to feel. Aristotle accepted the most ideal approach to move feeling starting with one individual then onto the next is through the expository gadget of narrating. Over 2,000 years after the fact, neuroscientists have discovered his proposition exact. Studies have discovered that accounts trigger a surge of neurochemicals in the cerebrum, quite oxytocin, the "ethical atom" that interfaces individuals on a more profound, passionate level.

In my investigation of 500 of the most well known TED Talks ever, I found that accounts made up 65% of the normal speaker's discussion, wheres 25% went to logos, and 10% went to ethos. At the end of the day, the triumphant equation for a mainstream TED talk is to envelop the huge thought by a story.

What sort of story? TED guardian, Chris Anderson, clarifies, "The narratives that can produce the best association are anecdotes about you actually or about individuals near you. Stories of disappointment, cumbersomeness, hardship, threat or debacle, told really, hurries profound commitment." The most close to home substance is the most relatable.

4) Metaphor

Aristotle accepted that similitude gives language its verbal excellence. "To be an ace of representation is the best thing by a wide margin," he composed. At the point when you utilize an illustration or similarity to contrast another thought with something that is natural to your crowd, it explains your thought by transforming the theoretical into something concrete.

How about we come back to the case of Warren Buffett, one of the savviest specialists of influence. Buffett once in a while gives a meeting without utilizing representation to come to his meaningful conclusion. At the point when you hear financial specialists state they search for organizations encompassed by a canal, for instance, it's a reference to a famous allegory he set up. Buffett has said more than once that he searches for organizations that are "monetary palaces" encompassed by canals that make it difficult for contenders to enter the business.

All the more as of late, Buffett gave a discourse at the 2017 Berkshire Hathaway yearly investors meeting, expressing that the development in medicinal services spending is the "tapeworm" of the American economy. Through this instinctive analogy, Warren precisely depicted a significant issue destroying the establishment of our monetary framework. Buffett didn't need to clarify what happens when the tapeworm becomes greater. Papers and websites covering the occasion utilized "tapeworm" in their title texts.

The individuals who ace the analogy can transform words into pictures that help other people increase a more clear comprehension of their thoughts — however more critically, recollect and share them. It is an incredible asset to have.

5) Brevity

Here once more, Aristotle was comparatively radical. "Aristotle had found that there are genuinely widespread cutoff points to the measure of data which any human can ingest and hold," composes Kings College teacher Edith Hall in Aristotle's Way. "With regards to influence, toning it down would be ideal."

Curtness is a pivotal component in delivering an influential discourse. A contention, Aristotle stated, ought to be communicated "as minimally and in as barely any words as could be expected under the circumstances." He additionally saw that the opening of an individual's discourse is the most significant since "consideration loosens wherever else instead of toward the start." The exercise here is: start with your most grounded point.

The uplifting news for communicators is that Aristotle accepted that influence can be educated. Truth be told, as per Hall, he was seen as "very undermining" to the political class in old Greece when he made the instruments of talk accessible to the majority. They needed to keep the recipe a firmly held mystery. However, Aristotle needed everybody to approach it. He supported that an individual's capacity to talk and compose well, and to utilize logical gadgets to change another's point of view, could release human potential and expand bliss. While the devices we use to convey thoughts have changed in the previous 2,000 years, the human mind has not. A similar equation that worked then will work now.

CHAPTER TWO:

USING SCARCITY TO CREATE VALUE FOR

YOURSELF AND BUSINESS

According to Wikipedia, "Scarcity is the essential monetary issue of having apparently boundless human needs in a universe of restricted assets. It expresses that society has inadequate gainful assets to satisfy every human need and needs. A typical misguided judgment on scarcity is that a thing must be significant for it to be rare, or the other way around."

Scarcity in the business world isn't having enough of the correct ability, assets and cash. For most, these kinds of restrictions can drive a business visionary to close or sell the business. For partnerships, pioneers might be compelled to convey monstrous representative cutbacks and spending decreases over all offices or potentially sell a failing to meet expectations working division to mollify investors and keep up an adequate organization advertise an incentive to fulfill the requests of Wall Street.

Pioneers that receive a scarcity attitude are the ones that are looking for the following best "layout" to drive manageable development and advancement. Sadly, very frequently most pioneers keep on concentrating on the current format for progress that their associations have been needy upon for a considerable length of time – one that is losing its effect and impact in the present quickly evolving territory. Pioneers aren't moving quick enough and subsequently – they are viewing the commercial center cruise them by. They are not associated with nor making the consuming stages that instant heads to become change operators for changing their plans of action. They smugly follow the state of affairs when what the association needs is a push to see through another focal point of chance.

Corporate pioneers in many cases wind up unconsciously mishandling the benefits accessible to them. Not out of unfaithfulness or flightiness – but since they have gotten excessively alright with approaching whatever assets they need. They gradually start to lose their serious edge in view of the plenitude around them that causes them to feel safe. In any case, is this bounty fake? Is it accurate to say that they are driving it properly?

At the point when pioneers have an excessive amount of access to assets, carelessness can dominate; unmerited benefits cover the need to lead with a shortage mindset.

We should figure out how to become hungry once more.

This beginnings with embracing the migrant point of view – the mentality that past ages had while encountering shortage and change on an undeniable level. A comparative soul of endurance, recharging and reevaluation – to see opportunity and beat misfortune before conditions power our hands – is the thing that the 21st century pioneer must epitomize in the event that we are to change the fate of the working environment, discover achievement in the commercial center, and recover our worldwide intensity in a changing and questionable world.

Why Scarcity Drives Us Wild

The Rule of Scarcity assumes a huge job in the influence procedure. Openings are in every case progressively important and energizing when they are rare and less accessible. We need to be the ones to possess the uncommon things or to get the keep going gadget on the rack. The more the shortage of a thing expands, the more the thing increments in esteem, and the more prominent the inclination to possess it.

At whatever point decision is restricted or undermined, the human need to keep up a portion of the constrained product causes us to want it considerably more. Shortage builds the estimation of any item or administration. Shortage drives individuals to activity, making us act rapidly because of a paranoid fear of passing up a chance. Possibly losing something before we've even had a chance to have it drives individuals to activity. We would prefer not to pass up anything we could have had. We need to get around any limitation put upon us. We feel unsettled and need back our opportunity. This causes pressure and agitation. The Rule of Scarcity relates to physical items, yet in addition to time, data, cost, and information.

The Threat of Potential Loss

Whenever somebody feels their opportunity — to pick, think, or act — is being limited, they "experience mental reactance and endeavor to reestablish their freedom."[3] With this limitation on opportunity we are headed to hook on to that thing which we dread will be confined much more. Rather than holding on and saying, "Alright, I'll surrender that," we adopt the contrary strategy. Out of nowhere, that limited thing is significantly progressively critical to us. Specialists call this inclination "reactance."[4] A strongly inspirational state, reactance makes us be enthusiastic, determined, or even nonsensical. We loathe feeling confined, so we are profoundly energetic to determine whatever makes that feeling. It is because of reactance that we demonstration, and that we need it now.

An examination including a gathering of male little children delineates exactly how ground-breaking the Rule of Scarcity is, even in extremely little youngsters. In the investigation, the little children were brought into a room that held two similarly energizing and engaging toys. A Plexiglas hindrance was set up with the goal that one of the toys sat close to it, while the other sat behind. The hindrance wasn't extremely tall, so a portion of the babies could essentially reach over the top and snatch for the toy.

For other people, however, the obstruction was still too high to even consider reaching over, so they could possibly arrive at that specific toy on the off chance that they went around and behind the Plexiglas. The scientists needed to check whether the blocked toy, being increasingly "rare," would draw more consideration and be progressively alluring.

The young men who could without much of a stretch reach over the top indicated no inclination toward the impeded or the unhindered toy; the unhampered toy was moved toward similarly as oftentimes and similarly as fast. For the young men who couldn't reach over the top, notwithstanding, the blocked toy was obviously the more alluring of the two — truth be told, the young men reached it multiple times quicker than with the unhindered toy![5] Even in little children, there was a desire to resist limitation of decision!

You Can't Have It

In another examination including youngsters, specialists told the kids they could choose from a wide cluster of pieces of candy. They at that point called attention to a specific piece of candy and revealed to them they ought not pick that one, however any of the others would be fine. The youngsters responded to the danger to their opportunity of decision by picking the bar they'd been advised not to choose. In doing as such, they believed they had safeguarded their opportunity to choose whatever bar they wanted.[6] It makes you wonder if that is additionally why Adam and Eve, who had the whole Garden of Eden to play in, couldn't avoid the prohibited natural product.

The Rule of Scarcity works since it causes individuals to feel like they will lose their chance to act and pick on the off chance that they don't do so right away. The danger of such misfortune makes earnestness in our dynamic. Have you at any point seen how individuals will in general be increasingly persuaded when confronted with conceivably losing something than when they may make strides voluntarily and gain something of equivalent worth?

Studies have checked this is a typical and reliable phenomenon.[7] For instance, do you figure mortgage holders would feel more direness to act on the off chance that they were told what amount of cash they would lose on the off chance that they didn't improve their protection, or in the event that they were told what amount of cash they would spare? They are bound to act in the event that they are told about their potential loss.

The psychological trigger of potential misfortune causes such extraordinary uneasiness in individuals that they demonstration to forestall the misfortune — despite the fact that they likely are not so much keen on the item itself. Envision settling on a choice where you have the entire day to decide and you have the consolation that when you return tomorrow, the thing will at present be accessible at a similar decent cost. You could take days to settle on that choice.

In any case, when shortage enters the image and you feel that the accessibility of the item, the planning, or even the cost will undoubtedly change without notice, the psychological trigger of shortage starts to work. You are headed to procure something to ease the danger of potential misfortune. That is the reason shoe sales reps continually bring you back the last pair of shoes accessible in your size at the deal cost — which closes today.

What we can't have is in every case more attractive and energizing than what we as of now have. As the aphorism says, "The grass is constantly greener on the opposite side of the fence." Any parent knows the aftereffect of telling a youngster she can't have or accomplish something.

The kid will quickly drop everything and need the one thing she can't have. Take a gander at Romeo and Juliet. The prohibited idea of their relationship made it much more grounded and additionally engaging them. Guardians should be forewarned about prohibiting their youngster's companions and darlings in light of the fact that the Rule of Scarcity will cause issues down the road for them.

The way wherein an item turns out to be rare likewise adds to making it progressively alluring. In a specific report, specialists gave subjects a treat container containing ten treats. At that point, taking the container back, the subjects were given another container containing just two treats. One gathering of subjects was told their treats had been offered away to different members on account of the interest for their examination. Another gathering was told their treats were removed on the grounds that the delegate had committed an error and had given them an inappropriate treat container. The outcomes showed that the treats that had gotten rare through social interest were appraised significantly higher than the treats that had gotten rare through the delegate's oversight. This, yet they were likewise the most exceptionally appraised of the considerable number of treats utilized in the study

The Rule of Scarcity works in any event, when the ideal article or thing won't generally advantage the beneficiary. A region in Florida ordered enactment disallowing the deal and utilization of clothing cleansers containing phosphates, as phosphates contrarily sway the earth and don't help clean the garments. Before the boycott became effective, stores encountered an expansion in deals of the phosphate-containing cleansers. After the boycott was in progress, stores inside the city saw a drop in clothing cleanser deals by and large, while stores in encompassing regions not influenced by the boycott saw an expansion in deals of the phosphate-containing cleansers.

Afterward, when purchasers were surveyed with regards to which cleansers were better, the inhabitants where the boycott had occurred evaluated the confined cleansers higher than any others in all classifications. The Rule of Scarcity had made the constrained item significantly more appealing.

The Rule of Scarcity in Marketing

Clinician Anthony Pratkanis of the University of California, Santa Cruz, is recorded as saying, "As customers we have a general guideline: If it is uncommon or rare, it must be important and acceptable."

Retail establishments utilize the Rule of Scarcity to snare buyers into a wild shopping free for all. Battles break out at retail establishments when individuals are pursuing those rare things, which are being offered at deal costs temporarily as it were. The lower costs are snare — a misfortune head for the store, however sure to produce a purchasing furor that is infectious. Blinded by shortage, shoppers will purchase everything without exception regardless of whether they needn't bother with it. For instance, you see supporters purchasing three DVD players. You ask them for what good reason "three," and they don't have the foggiest idea. All they know is that the store said supplies were constrained, the deal was distinctly for now, and every customer was restricted to three. So they purchased three DVD players.

—

71

A few stores have this "set number" thing down to flawlessness. Regularly when we go out on the town to shop, we are just calmly intrigued, telling the salesman, "Simply looking, much appreciated." We look over the bundling, analyze the deal sign, and so on.

At that point the salesman plays the number's down. Moving toward us, she says, "It's an extraordinary model, right? Particularly at this cost! Shockingly, I simply sold our last model." We abruptly feel frustrated. Presently that it's not, at this point accessible, we feel that we truly need it, despite the fact that we were just somewhat intrigued previously. We ask whether there may be another in the back or at another area. "All things considered, let me see what I can do. In the event that I can get another for you at this cost, will you take it?" she lures. Caught!

Interesting thing is, we don't understand the snare is being set, so the system has exactly the intended effect. We are approached to focus on an item when it appears as though it will before long be absolutely inaccessible, and subsequently appears to be amazingly alluring. Compromised with conceivably losing a lot, we concur. At that point, obviously, the sales rep returns with the extraordinary news. The item will be dispatched to the store in three days. Meanwhile, you should simply sign the deal.

We likewise observe the Rule of Scarcity being oftentimes utilized by home-shopping TV stations. They realize that uncommon things are exceptionally esteemed in our general public, so they generally have a little check running in the upper corner of the screen. You just have ten minutes to buy this valuable thing, and the clock tells you how brief period you have left to make this purchase of a lifetime. Home-shopping channels make time the rare asset.

They frequently have a counter on the screen as well. Now and again the counter runs down with each deal. So the host says, "We just have a predetermined number of these imported gadgets, and when they're completely gone, we will never sell them again." And the counter demonstrating the quantity of things remaining keeps on ticking down. The counter makes the impression of shortage.

Making a Demand: Can You Say "Constrained Supply"?

Have you at any point asked why some "in" cafés keep on having holding up lines outside? Long queues appear to make the eateries much progressively chic, expanding the length of the line by a significantly more noteworthy degree. For what reason don't eateries dispense with the holding up line by expanding their costs? They don't on the grounds that evacuating the lines would dispense with the shortage factor, and request would fall.

Consider how the Rule of Scarcity made the Beanie Baby marvel. When Ty Warner, the maker/engineer behind Beanie Babies, took certain Beanie Babies off the rack and restricted their accessibility, costs soar for the ceased and abruptly uncommon and important Beanies. Prodded on by the risk of missing out, authorities started storing the squishy toys and estimating with respect to which ones would be resigned next.

The Rule of Scarcity was additionally used to make interest for precious stones. Notwithstanding a sensational jump underway from 15 million carats to an astounding 100 million carats, DeBeers, the organization keeping up an imposing business model over jewel supply, despite everything figured out how to render the precious stones rare. Running just ten precious stone deals for every year and welcoming just a select number of sellers, DeBeers effortlessly controlled the stockpile and valuing. This, however each welcomed seller got just a constrained measure of jewels. DeBeers chose for them, and on the off chance that they whined, they were not welcomed back![12]

A proprietor of an effective hamburger bringing in organization chose to lead an investigation among his staff. The staff individuals were allocated to call the organization's clients and request that they buy meat in one of three different ways. One gathering of clients simply heard the standard introduction before providing their requests. Another gathering was given the standard introduction, yet they were likewise given proof that imported hamburger was relied upon to be hard to come by in the coming months. A third gathering was given the standard introduction just as the data about the meat's forthcoming shortage, however they were likewise informed that this news was not accessible to the overall population, and that the data gave was elite to the organization. As anyone might expect, the abrupt interest for meat made by these calls surpassed the stock available, and the organization needed to scramble to take care of the requests. Clients made aware of the coming shortage of the hamburger purchased twofold the measure of those accepting just the standard attempt to sell something, and those learning both of the coming shortage and this was "mystery data" purchased multiple times the sum as those meeting just the standard deals pitch![13]

What about when you take your youngster to be captured? They take ten distinct shots and afterward send you a proof for each. You're advised to choose the shots you like best and what number of duplicates of each you'd like. At that point, you're told the negatives will be obliterated inside a specific number of months. Obviously, you have an inclination that you would do well to get all the duplicates of the considerable number of shots you need now, or you won't have the option to later!

Making Allure

Consider when a lady needs to seem to be increasingly appealing to a specific man. In the event that she can set things up so she will simply happen to meet him while out on the town with some other fruitful, appealing man, at that point she will seem, by all accounts, to be more attractive than if she were only to meet only him at some club or bar. For sure in the event that you were selling land? You'd be savvy to have a few intrigued individuals along for the voyage through the property, since the enthusiasm of one customer will elevate the enthusiasm of another. Rather than your potential purchaser suspecting, "OK, I'm going to attempt to haggle here," he will think, "I would be wise to bounce or this other person will get it before I do!"

In one examination, understudies were given a composed portrayal of a specific novel. Half of the understudies' duplicates incorporated the depiction, "a book for grown-ups just, confined to those twenty-one years and over," while the other half contained no such limitation. When surveyed about their emotions about the novel, understudies finding out about the limitation showed that they figured they might want to peruse the book, while understudies who had not perused the limitation communicated altogether less interest.

Limiting access to data or material frequently makes it substantially more engaging. In spite of the fact that this theme ordinarily infers material of an explicitly unequivocal nature, shortage can apply to anything. Think about a type of control at the University of North Carolina. At the point when understudies discovered that a discourse for coed residences was prohibited, they turned out to be increasingly stricken with the possibility of coed dormitories. It is of extraordinary importance to understand that, while never having heard the real discourse, the oversight alone elevated the understudies' advantage. The understudies didn't have to hear the discourse to be convinced to help or become increasingly dedicated to the idea of coed dorms.

Reconsider the investigation directed by the University of Chicago Law School, The Rule of Obligation. The Rule of Scarcity was additionally busy working in this situation. At the point when the appointed authority decided that proof on the litigant's protection was forbidden, and in this manner must be ignored, the hearers really expanded the honor sum. The edited data was really grasped significantly more, hopping the harm installment by $13,000![16]

Extra Forms of Scarcity in Marketing

Consider the accompanying "shortage" strategies we see everyday:

- Clubs and cafés that make restrictive enrollment prerequisites
- Disney recordings and DVDs that are offered available to be purchased once at regular intervals
- Airlines that lone hold your seat for twenty-four hours, advising you that "These seats may sell out"

- Collectors who have practical experience in elusive collectibles and uncommon baseball cards
- Special "by greeting just" deals

- Going bankrupt deals
- Offers "not accessible" in stores
- Exclusive, once offers
- Memberships in a restrictive club

The most effective method to Use the Rule of Scarcity Some of the time shortage is important to assist us with settling on a choice.

The vast majority of us dread the purpose of settling on a choice, so we normally need to put it off and permit ourselves an opportunity to consider it. As a persuader, in any case, know that when your possibilities put off the choice, odds are they won't make one.

You could have the ideal item for them — something they truly need at this moment — however in the event that you let them go, they will most likely not return later and let you know, "OK, I at last chose. We should do it." Creating shortage enables your possibilities to settle on their choice. It likewise takes out the measure of time you squander finding possibilities who are as yet unsure about your item or administration. You can make genuine shortage with your item or administration without disregarding your ethics.

To make shortage, be certain you have the accompanying components solidly set up:

1.   Deadlines. Give your possibilities a cutoff time or a final turning point. We as a whole work on cutoff times at home and in our organizations. They are what cause us to make a move. On the off chance that there is no prompt motivation to make a move now, we won't. Numerous individuals don't take care of their tabs until they need to. According to the lines outside the mail station at 12 PM on April fifteenth, the majority of us don't pay our assessments until the latest moment possible. No cutoff time implies no activity.

2.	Limited Space, Numbers, or Access. In the event that your possibility feels like they are going after a restricted asset, they will be substantially more inspired to make a move. At the point when individuals dread they're going to pass up a lot, they feel an earnestness to act. Consider customers at closeout deals. They must speed over yonder and look at things before all the stuff is "picked over." Otherwise, with the store's restricted supplies, they'll miss the arrangement for eternity! This breaking point can likewise incorporate access to data. Our reaction to restricted data is a more noteworthy want to get that data and a more ideal viewpoint toward it than we had before the boycott was set up.

3.   Potential Loss. Possibilities must perceive that they may be constrained in their moves in the event that they don't make bit of leeway of your offer. Individuals will consistently exaggerate the thing you are confining. Make a condition of feeling wherein your possibility fears the misfortune. This is a staggering inclination they won't have the option to disregard. Spurred by limitation, this possibility turns into a sincerely inspired purchaser.

They won't be denied. The more you deny them, the more vitality you provide for your motivation. You have denied their entitlement to something, so they'll successfully have it. I can review events when I attempted to convince individuals not to buy a specific item since I sincerely felt it was not fitting.

The more I removed the item, the more they needed it. Consider every one of those sweepstakes messages that state, "You may as of now be a victor!" They used to state, "You can be a champ!" however the idea that you may as of now be a champ talked significantly more boisterously!

Do you figure individuals can discard such an envelope without opening it just to check and ensure? With the adjustment in motto, the sweepstakes organization encountered a checked increment in their reaction rates. Out of nowhere, individuals were apprehensive they may lose something they conceivably as of now had!

4.   Restrict Freedom. We need what we can't have. In the event that we are told a productisor will before long be inaccessible, we need it much more. Our craving goes up thus does the earnestness to act. Make a situation where you tell your possibility that the offer is just useful for such a long time. Reveal to them they need to act presently to make the most of the chance or they will miss out. This system works so well since we have all left offers like this previously, and they truly haven't been there when we returned. Stroll through leeway stores and you will see "Sold" signs on the furnishings. These signs make earnestness since another person has discovered an arrangement, thus should we.

In deals, this direness is known as the "remove" close. In the event that you accept away your possibilities' open door to engage with your item or administration, they normally need it more. This procedure additionally functions admirably when you need to check whether your possibility truly is keen on what you are giving. In the event that you are stuck and not certain how much time you need to go through with a possibility, or on the off chance that they are simply looking and not ready to settle on a choice, do a remove. On the off chance that they are genuinely keen on your item, they will liven up and turn out to be increasingly intrigued. If not, they will leave. In any case, you have spared yourself time and vitality.

Why shortage works (FOMO, putting on a show, and the sky is the limit from there)

One of the most notable shortage contemplates was directed by Stephen Worchel in 1975. He and his associates offered subjects treats in a container. One container had 10 treats, and the other container had two.

Subjects favored the treats from the container with two in it, despite the fact that the treats in the two containers were indistinguishable.

two containers with various quantities of treats to outline shortage study.

From that point forward, much research has bolstered the viability of shortage in the promoting scene too.

For instance, a 2015 research paper notes;

When something is uncommon, it's appealing—genuine whether you're discussing valuable gemstones or an unblemished release of the principal issue of Action Comics (which presented Superman). What's more, therapists have since a long time ago realized that on the off chance that you can make a customer decent increasingly alluring by causing it to seem uncommon.

Why would that be? Quite a bit of it originates from the dread of passing up a great opportunity (FOMO). FOMO is characterized as an "inescapable fear that others may be having compensating encounters from which one is missing. It is described by the 'want to remain consistently associated with what others are doing.'"

As you'll see from the models underneath, shortage is vigorously predicated on the possibility that others want the item/administration, and that so as to get in on the products, you've gotta act now.

It's not constantly a basic capacity of FOMO, in any case. We appear to fear topsy-turvy control also—it's the reason you need what you can't have.

For instance, there was an examination in which ladies were demonstrated a photo of their latent capacity dream man. A large portion of the ladies were told the person was single, and the other half were old he was seeing someone.

The outcomes: 59% said they would be keen on seeking after the single person, yet that number bounced to 90% when they thought he was taken.

On the off chance that something is uncommon or out of reach, we need it more.

Indeed, even Aristotle noticed the joy of irregularity, commenting

that is the reason what comes to us just at long interims is wonderful, regardless of whether it be someone or something; for it is a change from what we had previously, and, additionally, what comes just at long interims has the estimation of irregularity.

On the off chance that something isn't rare, at that point it isn't wanted or esteemed that much. Gestures of recognition from an instructor who only here and there acclaims are esteemed more than acclaims from an educator who is liberal with their applause.

Shortage is non-direct procedure. As something turns out to be all the more rare or less rare, the longing for it doesn't change in a proportionate manner.

In the case of everything is rare, at that point shortage itself comes up short on its worth and individuals become excessively accustomed to it. Investigations of retail deals have demonstrated that if more than about 30% of products have "deal" sticker on them, the adequacy of this strategy diminishes.

Human conduct is with the end goal that we are likelier to buy something in case we're educated that it's the absolute last one or that a unique arrangement will before long lapse. Point is, if individuals truly accept that they'll be passing up something, they'll be provoked to act all the more rapidly to get it.

At the point when shortage works (and when it doesn't)

Shortage doesn't generally work, however. It is anything but a silver slug.

For example, scientists appeared in four examinations that shortage has a more grounded beneficial outcome on item assessment when:

- Remarkable quality of influence information is low;
- Recurrence of introduction to shortage claims is low;
- Choice reversibility is high;
- Subjective burden is high.

Fundamentally, if individuals have a higher information on influence strategies or more presentation to shortage claims, they're less inclined to esteem a rare item more.

This examination found that "when shoppers deciphered shortage guarantees as a business strategy, the constructive outcome of shortage asserts on item assessment would be weakened."

To summarize, if the shortage is BS—and your clients are keen—it's going to hurt more than help.

shortage models that work

There are commonly two kinds of shortage you can use to expand deals:

Amount related shortage (e.g., "Two seats left at this price!");

Time-related shortage (e.g., "A day ago to buy!").

We scoured the Internet and discovered 18 genuine instances of shortage. Most likely you can discover motivation for your own execution. For the sake of entertainment (and as a wake up call) we additionally discovered some flinch commendable instances of shortage.

1. Booking.com

Booking.com does numerous things well, one of them being shortage. Investigate an item for inns in Dublin: instances of shortage on booking.com pages.

Presently, there are a couple of shortage triggers having an effect on everything here:

"Booked multiple times for your dates over the most recent 24 hours on our site," which reveals to you this lodging is alluring.

"Just 6 rooms left on our site," which proposes that time is heading out to book.

"See our last accessible rooms," adds shortage to the source of inspiration.

There's a genuine breaking point to lodgings as there's a sure amount accessible. Approval to booking.com for showing this data precisely, unmistakably, and powerfully.

2. Amazon.com

You have, obviously, shopped on Amazon. What's more, I'm certain you've seen the admonition of "just X left in stock":

case of restricted stock on Amazon.

This, in mix with the criticalness play for transportation ("Want it tomorrow?"), is a compelling method for getting me to make a move and maintain a strategic distance from the loss of that uncommon book I had my eye on.

3. Chubbies Shorts

I'm a Chubbies fanboy. Their advertising is excellent. From their duplicate to their marking to their social nearness, they slaughter it. What's more, they utilize "restricted time" item shortage.

Here's a case of an advancement they run every year called Fourth of Julyber:

case of time-restricted shortage by a garments retailer.

Fundamentally, they discharge an "unconditional present" each hour with a buy. This unconditional present is temporarily—accessible just on that day, at that particular hour. In this way, in the event that you need an American Flag speedo, act rapidly.

4. Chubbies Pt. 2

Chubbies likewise does an incredible time sensitive shortage play here:

time sensitive shortage for shorts.

At the point when I think Chubbies, I frequently consider fourth July. Furthermore, they discharge an exceptional thing for pre-deal with the assurance that it will show up directly before the fourth.

By making a move now, you won't pass up the consideration you'll get from wearing these great 5" inseam shorts.

5. Think Geek

Another case of topical shortage is something I found on Think Geek (which, unfortunately, moved its activities back to parent organization GameStop in 2019).

It's difficult to peruse, yet the pennant says, "There's still time for Mother's Day conveyance w/sped up delivery" (for all you a minute ago customers).

case of shortage with standard on landing page.

CONCLUSION

"Neuro-phonetic writing computer programs" is a promoting term for a "science" that two Californians— Richard Bandler and John Grinder—thought of during the 1970s. Bandler was a stoner understudy at UC Santa Cruz (simply like I later was during the 00s), at that point a famous hub for hallucinogenics, hipsters and radical reasoning (presently a world renowned hub for Silicon Valley hopefuls).

Processor was at the time a partner educator in phonetics at the college (he had recently filled in as a Captain in the US Special Forces and in the insight network, ahem not excessively this, you know, is significant... aheh...). Together, they worked at demonstrating the methods of Fritz Perls (author of Gestalt treatment), family specialist Virginia Satir and, above all, the supernaturally talented subliminal specialist Milton Erickson.

Bandler and Grinder looked to dismiss quite a bit of what they saw as the insufficiency of talk treatment and slice directly to the core of what methods really attempted to create conduct change. Propelled by the PC transformation—Bandler was a software engineering major—they additionally looked to build up a mental programming language for individuals.

What they thought of was a sort of development of hypnotherapy—while old style trance relies upon procedures for placing patients into interesting dazes (even to the point of losing awareness on order), NLP is considerably less cumbersome: it's a system of layering inconspicuous importance into communicated in or composed language so you can embed recommendations into an individual's oblivious psyche without them recognizing what you're doing.

There is a likelihood that in the event that you have searched out this book, you might be having a few battles or dissatisfactions with uneasiness.

In case you're having these battles, you're not the only one! 33% of the populace will build up a type of uneasiness issue inside their lifetimes and, moreover, almost a similar sum will have grievances about their primary care physician and their strategy for treatment. Along these lines, in case you're searching for an elective alternative, look no further!

To start with, it's critical to see precisely what is causing your nervousness. Your uneasiness depends on something you're apprehensive about and its results. For instance, on the off chance that you have social nervousness, you may fear what conceivable awful things can transpire when you're in a social situation. Another significant part of your tension that is imperative to comprehend is that in spite of the fact that there might be and most likely are, straightforward answers for whatever your dread might be, you rather decide to consider vainglorious arrangements that are totally ridiculous.

Your absolute first system with regards to tension is to reframe your nervousness and the side effects you're encountering. To do this, image yourself having an ordinary episode of tension and what that resembles for you. For instance, you have tension when your beau or spouse is late getting back home. You've shown up home, it gets late, he isn't home yet, he hasn't called and you start having uneasiness contemplating where he may be, what he may be doing, who he may be with and you persuade preposterous thoughts, similar to he is failing to come home again and he is most likely undermining you.

There are a couple of elements here. To start with, you have to concur and grappled with the way that you have made the tension and your frenzy. You're the person who got all worked up and started disclosing to yourself these things. Is there or was there ever any genuine, authentic verification for any of your musings? Odds are, the appropriate response is no. Assuming this is the case, you have recently recognized your first issue. Presently, think about your procedure. What point of view drove you to accepting these things? What did you let yourself know? Are these things grounded in realities? Or on the other hand, would you say you are causing things to up and making a hasty judgment? Consider your line of reasoning during your nervousness and recognize the great and the terrible.

Moreover, inquire as to whether you could clarify this line of reasoning to another person. In the event that you can, you have now recognized another issue. This is on the grounds that you are so certain about these things that are causing you tension that you have persuaded yourself so much that you could likewise persuade someone else. That is the manner by which profoundly you have gone overboard. It's critical to recognize this hurtful procedure. Next, consider this equivalent circumstance that is causing you nervousness and discussion about it so anyone can hear however, this time, as though you're watching another person do it.

Does this appear to be sensible and like an ordinary point of view? Odds are, your answer is no. Presently, you have completely acknowledged, from numerous perspectives, why this manner of thinking that is causing your nervousness is causing you so much disappointment and pessimism. You currently need to instruct yourself to pick an alternate manner of thinking. You can do this through self-talking yourself through various situations and picking positive lines of reasoning as opposed to negative.

The following system you can use to handle your uneasiness issues is by accomplishing something many refer to as getting to assets and getting to arrangements. In many cases, there are occasions or certain things throughout your life that trigger your nervousness. This strategy centers around that trigger and encourages you to adapt to how this trigger and the circumstance causes you to feel just as how you can explain this. In the first place, you have to recognize your concern and its trigger.

For instance, perhaps grinding away, when your supervisor addresses you in an exceptionally short manner it makes nervousness for you since you feel like the person resents you or treating you unreasonably. Since you've pinpointed the issue, it's an ideal opportunity to handle it. You can do this by asking yourself a progression of inquiries. For instance, "What would you like to accomplish by explaining this problem,""What need to happen to cause you to feel assuaged and like this issue is tackled?" Or, "In what manner will you realize this issue is solved,""If and when this issue is comprehended, how and what will you feel? Answer these inquiries genuinely and consider the appropriate responses.

You may begin to understand that you've responded to many inquiries for yourself, particularly concerning how you can take care of your concern just by investigating it with those inquiries. Next, you will ask yourself another arrangement of inquiries. This time, you need to consider times when the issue that prompts your tension isn't going on.

At that point, ask yourself the accompanying inquiries: "What are the occasions when you feel the issue isn't as awful or doesn't exist by any stretch of the imagination?" What were you doing around then? Is it accurate to say that you were doing anything another way than you generally do or anything strange? You may understand that with these inquiries, your eyes are opened to times when your tension is lessoned and perhaps nonexistent. On the off chance that you wind up understanding this, emphasis on your conduct as of now and how you can instruct yourself to have that conduct all the more reliably.

In any case, in the event that you find that this second arrangement of inquiries doesn't concern you, move onto one final arrangement of what is alluded to as "wonder questions." For instance: "Envision, one night, as your resting profoundly, that the issue or issues that cause your uneasiness have mysteriously or by some supernatural occurrence has been explained. You have no clue how this issue was settled, since you were profound sleeping yet when you wake up, how would you know the issue or issues have been illuminated? What's unique? What parts with it? This may offer you a few responses to how you have to change your line of reasoning or demeanor to roll out this improvement occur and stay away from your nervousness.

Another procedure you can utilize is daze and figuring out how to use unwinding stays.

The absolute first approach to do this is to educate and prepare yourself to quit utilizing and tighteningcertain muscle bunches that cause you to be increasingly tense and therefore, progressively on edge. A portion of these essential muscle gatherings may be your stunning, the muscles in your brow and holding your hands. On the off chance that you wind up becoming on edge or encountering the issues you for the most part do when your uneasiness introduces itself, take one moment to check these muscle gatherings. It is safe to say that they are flexed and fixed? Provided that this is true, take one moment to fix this and afterward perceive how you feel!

You may not understand how huge of a distinction this may make in your tension levels! Next, focus and spotlight on you're out breathing as opposed to when you take in. At the point when your body encounters nervousness, it's normal to animate and worry your internal breathing developments. Rather than permitting this to occur, center around breathing out in a quiet, loosening up way. This may assist with quieting you down in the event that you'reexperiencing nervousness. In conclusion, you need to concentrate on the psychological symbolism you have in your mind.

As people, we spend an enormous segment speaking with ourselves inside our heads. This correspondence incorporates mental symbolism and in many cases, individuals who experience nervousness on various levels have negative mental pictures that they are taking care of and making for themselves. Train yourself and your psyche to maintain a strategic distance from this. To do this, you can begin preparing yourself every day.

For instance, consistently, follow along and know about what mental pictures are coming into your psyche. At the point when you experience a negative one, promptly shut down it and supplant it with a positive one. This will take a considerable amount of self-talk and self-restraint however in the event that you focus on it and preserver, you will be shocked and please with exactly the amount of your nervousness and figuring you can change!

At long last, one final procedure you can use for any tension you're encountering in your life is through something many refer to as tying down. This is likewise like traditional molding. The whole purpose of this strategy includes finding what outer prompt is trigging an inside reaction and figuring out how to change this outside signal to then change your reaction.

For instance, you have an extreme dread of monkeys and when you see monkeys, you become inside terrified and alarmed. This triggers your tension. To change this conduct, you need to prepare yourself to make a connection between the outer sign and the inner feeling. To do this, you need to relate whatever the signal might be with something positive as opposed to negative.

In this way, for instance, in the event that you have a dread of monkeys, you would need to prepare your brain to connect seeing monkeys with something you truly love, for instance, your kids or you most loved memory rather than a surge of frightening made up results regarding what may happen when you interact with monkeys. Or then again, you can even pick an article to change the passionate connection to the signal. For instance, when you see the image of monkeys, you can pick an article that you enormously associate with or something that implies a great deal to you and focus on that to maintain a strategic distance from the negative feeling that triggers your nervousness.

You can in any event, carry this item with you to genuinely take a gander at it and spotlight on it as opposed to concentrating on the feelings of dread, outrage or trouble. One other way you can utilize mooring is however solid affiliation. Similarly likewise with the last pervious alternatives, you can think about a sound that implies a great deal to you or that you partner numerous cheerful recollections with and utilize that to help control the feelings that trigger your nervousness. For instance, when you see monkeys or pictures of monkeys you can attempt to think about the sound of your granddad's voice or the sound of your infant snickering.

You can prepare your mind to think about these things rather than dread and hence, transform your upsetting feelings into cheerful ones. At long last, the last instrument you can use for securing is the possibility of a significant relationship to battle any negative emotions. At the point when you see the prompt to whatever causes the trigger, you need to prepare your brain to think about the positive, upbeat relationship you have picked rather than your negative feelings.

.

CPSIA information can be obtained
at www.ICGtesting.com
Printed in the USA
BVHW041400110621
609350BV00013B/3242